# Plants to Gro

## How to start a profitable business

Copyright 2012; Geoff Buckley

Published by Castelen Press

3 Golfcourse Road, Mt.Tamborine

Queensland 4272, Australia

Website: www.growinghealthyorganicfood.com

Third edition

Published January 2012

ISBN: 978-0-9808395-2-4

1

## Bonus Offer.

You now have some valuable information if you want to grow fruit & vegetables for an income. This book shows you how to make money in a few weeks e.g. you can grow radishes and rocket in 4 or 5 weeks! However you then need to be able to sell them. This book identifies 12 crops that are easy and quick to grow **and** that are highly saleable i.e. in good demand. They have been selected for each of the main climate zones. Some grow in more than one climate zone.

It also tells you how to grow them!

If you like this book, you might be interested in trying a training course I have put together that has the results of an 18 month study on the profitability of over 100 different crops, covering fruits, nuts, berries, vegetables and herbs. Initially I did this based on retail prices but it now includes wholesale buying prices, because if you grow a crop in any significant volume it is hard to sell it at retail prices.

If you are interested go to www.growinghealthyorganicfood.com and click on "Training course 2" to find out more. If you decide you want to do the program enter coupon code "HOWTO77" and you will get 33% off the normal price of the course as **a special bonus offer for buying this book.**

## Foreword

### 1. Introduction

(a) Why food prices are set to rise.

(b) Why I advocate you grow organically

(c) Reasons why growing small food crops is an increasingly profitable business to be in.

### 2. Key factors affecting profitability

(a) How much money can I expect to make?

(b) What price will I get?

(c) Who will I sell to?

### 3. Choice of Crops: A key factor

(a) Selecting a suitable crop based on profitability

(b) Choice of crops based on climate zones, growing times and consumer demand

Information on seed quantities needed per given area.

### 4. General Growing Principles

(a) Water

(b) Plant Food

(c) Soil preparation

(d) Building organic matter

(e) Fertility maintenance

(f) Weed control

## 5. Which crops will I grow?

(a) Growing methods

(b) Propagating seeds

(c) Spacing of seeds/seedlings and when to plant

(d) Suitable crops for tropical climates: button squash, eggplant, capsicum, watermelon

(e) Suitable crops for warm temperate climates: basil, beans, beetroot, carrots

(f) Suitable crops for cool temperate climates: radish, mint, spinach(silver beet), broccoli

## 6. Marketing

(a) Marketing Factors

(b) Sell retail not wholesale

(c) Incorporate DIY sales into your operation


**7. Develop a plan and implement it**

(a) Examples of how to make $50,000 in 4 months.

(b) Labour required.


**8. Investment options**


**9. Conclusion**

# Foreword.

This book is based on three simple lessons I have learned since I wrote my first book:

1.  Fruit & nut trees take a minimum of 3 years before you earn a cent and then you get generally only one crop a year.

2.  The typical growing cycle for vegetables & herbs is two to three months and you can often get three to five crops a year (depending on your climate zone).

3.  Bad weather (such as strong winds & hail or 2 to 3 months of persistent rain with no sunshine) can wipe out a year's income with fruit & nuts; with most vegetables & herbs you can recover in 3 months.

When I wrote my first book called "Growing Healthy," I suggested that to achieve the sub-title of "How to make over $100,000 p.a on five acres" you should allocate 4 acres to fruit trees and 1 acre to vegetables & herbs.

Subsequently, after two years of extensive research and trials, I found to my amazement that it was possible to make $50,000 in 3 to 4 months on half an acre. With the right climate this can be scaled up to $150,000 p.a. in one year by doing it 3 times. If you were then to extend this to one acre you could make $300,000 p.a. on one acre in one year. This is three times as much in one fifth of the land!! Of course this requires a favourable climate and it will take more labour.

I felt my readers of book 1 deserved to be let into this insight and thus I wrote my second book.

**Disclaimer**: earnings achieved depend on the skills and experience of the grower, the vagaries of the weather, being able to sell all that is produced and the selling prices obtained.

# Plants to Grow

## (How to start a profitable business).

## 1.Introduction.

### (a) Why food prices are set to rise.

One of the reasons growing vegetables and/or herbs is a good business strategy is that food prices are rising dramatically; in fact in 2010 we have already seen some significant price rises and food shortages. Here in S.E.Queensland I have seen the price of onions rise from $20 per 20 kilogram bag to $80. Partly this is the result of a very wet season, which can be explained by climate change extremes which aren't going to settle down any time soon. Organically grown carrots were unobtainable in this region for nearly six months. We are now being paid wholesale prices of $9 per kilogram for organically grown beans. Last year we received just $5. This is an 80% increase in just 12 months. What other investments have risen that fast?

The world population is already 6.5 billion and is projected to reach 9 billion by 2050. There is a finite amount of land and water and already many people are dying of starvation and more have little water; the situation can only get worse.

All agriculture depends on oil but conventional agriculture depends to a massive extent on huge quantities of oil and gas for transport, harvesting, cultivation, fertilizers and herbicides and pesticides.  As oil reserves decline, prices of oil will rise further and faster.  If you need to be persuaded that Peak Oil is a reality, there is one set of statistics that is totally convincing.  In the 1960's the world consumed 4 billion barrels of oil per year and the average rate of discovery annually, was around 30 billion barrels.  Now, we consume 30 billion barrels of oil per year and the discovery rate is approaching 4 billion barrels of crude per year.  Oil reserves are diminishing but developing countries like China & India are using more and more oil and gas and most westernized countries are still addicted to oil.  This guarantees that the oil price will rise and that there will soon be shortages of oil & gas.  Food prices will rise even more steeply than they have already as this happens.  As oil prices rise farmers have no choice but to start switching to organic farming methods that use less oil. Many do not know how to do this and the degradation of soil that has occurred with chemical farming practices will make it impossible to do within a short time frame.

## (b)  Why I advocate growing organically.

When oil prices rise and oil become a scarce commodity, farmers will not have a choice as to what sort of farming methods they need to adopt. Farmers will have to convert to small farms or gardens because they are far more productive per acre than conventional large farms particularly when energy prices rise. We saw this happen in Cuba when they had an oil embargo and had to change their food production methods.

The other major reason for growing organically is that conventional farming methods are not viable over the longer term. They destroy soil structure and soil life. They demand the use of toxic herbicides and pesticides to combat the insects and diseases that are a consequence of chemical farming practices. These problems are increasing in severity every year in spite of the fact that ever increasing quantities of highly destructive chemicals are being used. The major constituent of herbicides is glyphosate and Professor Don Huber (emeritus professor of plant pathology) produced a report in Dec/Jan 2010 the key findings of which are "The widespread use of glyphosate is causing negative impacts on soil and plants as well as possibly animal and human health."(www.fourwinds10.com).

# (c ) Why this book will convince you that growing crops is an increasingly profitable business to be in.

There is a great variation in the profitability of different crops. This variability applies to categories such as vegetables, herbs, berries, nuts and fruit and to individual crops within each of the categories. A few crops are even unprofitable to grow when you take into account labour, fertilizer inputs, planting and harvesting costs.

Profitability also depends to a large extent on production methods. Generally we have been told that to be profitable, one must grow on a large scale. Things are changing.

One thing that is generally not realised is that small farms are far more profitable than large farms when you look at production per acre as opposed to production per person. Profitability of large scale production units drops dramatically when you add in the increasing cost of energy. Energy prices have been ignored as a major input cost for many decades. This is about to change dramatically.

Over the past 15 months, I have analysed the profitability of over 100 food crops. From this study, I have selected a group of profitable crops and come up with a step-by-step plan showing you how to make a lot of money in 3 to 4 months. You will be absolutely amazed at just how much money it is possible to make on a relatively small area of land, in a short period of time.

This is absolutely **unique** information. No other book contains this information.

This report provides a framework for you to get started quickly. Growing successfully depends on your skill as a farmer, your knowledge of the uniqueness of each crop's characteristics, your ability to manage the necessary inputs to ensure soil balance and soil health, and your preparedness to follow an implementation plan. To provide all this information is beyond the scope of this introductory report. Here I cover, for example, only 12 crops out of a possible list of well over 100. However, we do provide a far more comprehensive range of products & services which can provide you with much more depth and detail if you wish to take it further. (See www.growinghealthyorganicfood.com ).

Of course having this information won't make you a lot of money unless you also have the skills and know how to put this information into action. However, I am going to share with you my detailed knowledge of how to grow the crops that I have identified as being some of the most profitable crops you can grow if you want to make money quickly.

Some crops are much easier to sell than others. People buy and eat potatoes and carrots every day. With this in mind, I have chosen crops that are generally easy to sell.

## 2. Key factors affecting profitability.

Clearly your **choice of crops** is fundamental to your success. Other factors you have to evaluate are **market demand** for the crops you select, **your ability to access that market quickly, cheaply and with minimal effort**, and your ability to do what you have set out to do: grow crops. Successful growing will depend on your **knowledge about how to grow your crops.** Surprisingly, one of the factors you might think is vitally important is **soil fertility**, but this is not a big factor. Even poor soil can be turned into highly productive land relatively quickly and without a huge cost provided you are working on a small scale. Turning a worn out, humus depleted 1,000 acre farm into a profitable enterprise is an extremely expensive exercise but when you start small, you can do it without great expense but it will take work and some scrounging to find the inputs you need to improve the fertility of your soil without spending a lot of money.

Far more important than soil fertility, is **location**. You could take a burnt-out inner city factory site and turn it into a prosperous farm more easily than you could a 1,000-acre farm that is 500 miles from the nearest town. In fact we know someone who is doing just this in down-town Los Angeles. Inspired by what we have done he has set up an inner city farm on part of a warehouse block to grow vegetables for his family's restaurant.

How you grow is important.  The techniques you use, the infrastructure you have, the degree of mechanization and the cost of energy input all affect profitability.  In the initial stages, the time it takes between planting and harvesting your crop will make a difference as will turnaround time between harvesting and replanting the next crop. When you harvest and replant the same day, which can be done if you use the strategies we advocate, then your profits really start to escalate.

Some crops take far less time to grow than others and when you factor in time, it makes a huge difference in terms of profitability.  This is why crop selection is so important.  Many crops are not profitable and some others are only marginally profitable, particularly when the cost of land, buildings & machinery are taken into account.

Ideas about farming are changing rapidly with increasing costs of energy and decreasing costs of labour.  Substituting labour for mechanisation, which was completely unthinkable only 5 or 10 years ago, is now becoming a increasingly viable proposition especially if you do things the smart way and reduce the amount of labour needed by clever growing strategies.

Labour costs per crop do vary and some crops are more labour intensive than others. The fact is that beans take a long time to pick by hand. Carrots are easy to grow but they are difficult to prepare for sale when you have to wash and bunch them by hand. Labour costs are also affected by the expertise, enthusiasm and skill of the people involved. Inexperienced or unfit people will take 3 -5 times longer to do a job that others can do when they know what they are doing and have lots of energy and strength.

Other important factors are the price you get, the yield you get per given area and the production costs. Price depends very much on the quality of your produce and HOW you sell it. You receive a much higher price if you sell direct to the end consumer.

The main running costs include water, irrigation, mulch, seeds or seedlings, fertilizers, electricity and labour. The big capital costs are the land, buildings and machinery used.

## (a) What sort of profit will I make?

Profitability will depend to a large extent on:

> (i) Cost of inputs: land, labour, fertilizer and compost, energy, infrastructure, water, machinery and tools.

> (ii) Yield per acre (which depends largely on your growing skills & experience)

> (iii) Turn-around time for each crop

> (iv) Costs incurred in marketing, transport, packing and wastage.

Your income will vary from crop to crop (and according to the weather and variety you choose to grow). The good news is that before costs you could make approximately  $20 to $100 per crop per month per 100 square feet of land (or 10 sq.metres). This may not sound much but if you scale it up, it becomes over $8000 to $40,000 per acre **per month** (as one acre is 43,560 sq.ft. or 435.6 x100 sq.ft.). That's a lot of money.  In our business plan (see chapter 7) we grow over a two month to four month period and show you how to make $50,000 selling at wholesale prices.

How much you make per year depends on the nblength of the growing season.  If you live in a cold area, your growing season might be between 4 and 7 months and you will be able to grow only one or two crops on the same land in that period depending on the growing time for the crops you select. If you live in a warm temperate or sub-tropical climate the growing season can be as long as 10 or 12 months. This means you can grow up to four crops on the one area of land in a year. You can of course, extend the growing season in a cold climate by investing in a greenhouse and in tropical or temperate area you can extend growing seasons by putting in a shade house, which reduces the impact of hot sun in mid-summer.

**(b) What price will I get?**

Price depends very much on the quality of your produce and how you sell it. You receive a much higher proportion of the consumer buying price if you sell direct to the end customer. Middlemen, agents, transport and packaging can take a large proportion of your profits unless you develop do-it-yourself strategies. As we mentioned at the beginning of this paper, prices are rising..... fast. You can look forward to an activity that is generating increasing revenue, and increasing profits.

## (c) Who shall I sell to?

At the beginning our production far exceeded our initial expectations and early on we discovered the problem that comes from having to sell 1,000 beautiful, large, organically grown cabbages. They were so large that we could only fit a few into the car we then owned so it wasn't economical to transport them long distances. Cabbages are not a hugely sought after vegetable where we live.

This experience provided a huge learning and provided the incentive to start up a small, local, community owned market where we could sell whatever we grew without having to seek out buyers and without incurring high transport costs. The market makes sure that we can sell everything we grow. Sometimes you have to start thinking outside the box when it comes to sales strategies.

So... the first thing you need to do, ideally before you even start growing, is to find a market and if there isn't one, think about creating your own. Sell from your front gate, get a stall at a local market, visit businesses and restaurants nearby, create a box scheme and supply the employees of a local factory. Ask your neighbours. You may be surprised to find that your market is actually right next door. After all, everyone eats don't they? So all you need is people and there are lots of them around.

# 3. Choice of Crops - a key factor

### (a) Selecting a crop depending on climate and profitability

Deciding which crops you grow is critical to your initial success. Don't do as I did and grow cabbages without first checking out whether or not you can sell them!

I'm a mathematician by training. Numbers matter. I like analysing things and I have spent two years analysing the profitability of growing crops. We've been doing it for 14 years as a "retirement" activity so I know that it is possible to make quite a lot of money. The numbers stack up. It is an extremely profitable exercise.

I've done the hard work for you. I've analysed over 100 crops and ranked them in terms of profitability. The ones I suggest you grow will make a good profit. These are carefully selected based on my 14 years experience and a detailed analysis of which crops are more profitable. They meet the important criteria of being crops that people want. I don't recommend you grow cabbages to start with!

I strongly recommend you grow all four of the nominated crops for your climate zone to diversify your risk.

Climate is the primary factor in deciding which crops you can grow. Temperature has a major impact on growth. When it is too hot or too cold, growth stops dead in its track for most plants. If you are in an area that gets extremely hot temperatures (over 30 degrees Celsius) you can improve production by using a shade house in summer. Depending on the size of the area you have under cultivation this can be a small homemade device with shade cloth draped over wood or plastic poles, or a large walk-in shade house with sprinklers.

If you live in a cold climate that gets lots of snow, you can improve productivity and lengthen your growing season by using a greenhouse in winter.

**(b) Suitable crops for different climate zones.**

The crops I have selected for each climate are:

| Tropical Crops. | No.of weeks growing time | Approx. no. of seeds per ounce |
|---|---|---|
| Buttonsquash | 7 | 1000 |
| Eggplant | 10 | 6500 |
| Capsicums | 10.5 | 4500 |
| Water melons | 11.5 | 250 large variety/550 small variety |

NB You will find that buttonsquash (or patty pan) are the most profitable of these.

| Temperate Climate Crops | | |
|---|---|---|
| Basil | 7 | 12,000 |
| Runner beans | 6 to 12 | 100 |
| Beetroot | 8.5 | 1550 |
| Carrots | 10 | 22,000 |

Don't overlook basil; the only problem with basil is finding a market for it. If you can find a good market for herbs there is a lot of money to be made; try hotels, bed & breakfast places.

| Cold Climate Crops | | |
|---|---|---|
| Radish | 3 to 6 | 3000 |
| Mint | 7 | Not planted from seeds |
| Spinach | 6.5 | 2500 |
| Broccoli | 8.5 | 9000 |

Radishes have one of the shortest growing times of any crop that I have studied.

You will find spinach and radishes the most profitable of these crops but don't overlook mint; the only problem with mint is finding a market for it. If you can find a good market for herbs there is a lot of money to be made; try hotels, bed & breakfast places.

N.B. The exact growing time will depend on the weather and also varies with the different varieties.

The above crops have also been selected for a short growing time ie from 6 to 12 weeks. This guarantees a quick financial return on your investment.

# 4.How to grow -- general principles

The place you grow needs sunshine and water.

In summer vegetables need water daily and in winter 2 or 3 days a week (when its not raining!), so your source of water is important. The minimum need is a water tank nearby that provides water for a watering can or for sprinklers. A dam, river or water bore could also be big pluses.

**(a) Water**

Your major requirements are sunshine and water. Without these, nothing will grow.

Your soil needs good drainage so a small slope is ideal. If drainage is a problem, it is a good investment to dig a trench at least one foot deep along the high side, put gravel and an agricultural pipe in it with more gravel on top. Finally replace the soil. With this type of drain you can remove excess water and take it into an area where it won't cause problems.

In summer you vegetables will need water daily. In winter you should water 2 or 3 days per week when it doesn't rain. Having a reliable source of water is really important.

If you live in dry areas, there are many ways to minimise water requirements but information like that is beyond the scope of this book.

Town water is not ideal because it contains chemicals such as chlorine and fluoride and if you use town water, it is a good idea to filter it. Town water supplies are often costly. A better solution is to harvest the water from your own roof and install water tanks or a pond. If you have a river, dam or bore you have a great asset when it comes to growing small crops.

## (b) Plant food

Plants require food to grow. I'm not talking about any food. They need ample quantities of the right food.

In general this should come from the soil, but frequently soils do not have the amount or correct balance of the food that plants need. Soils that have been intensively cultivated using chemical fertilizers, weedicides and pesticides will certainly not support a healthy crop. The good news is that they can be made fertile and productive but you need to know how.

How do you know what sort of food is in the soil that you plan to use for growing your plants?

You do a soil test. A soil test provides you with all the information you need to know what inputs you require to keep your plants healthy and growing well. A soil test identifies mineral deficiencies and excesses, the level of organic matter. Without the correct minerals in your soil your plants will be diseased and stunted and prone to insect attack. Without organic matter there will be no soil micro-organisms which are absolutely essential if you want to grow healthy crops. Soil test provide you with essential information that you need to make important decisions.

The quality of your soil will determine how quickly you can start growing. You can add fertilizers, humus and manure but if the soil is grossly deficient in one or more major elements, it will take a while for the micro-organisms to get to work and break down the fertilizers into plant-available food. Micro-organisms are key to successful growing of crops. They are key to all the processes that take place within the soil. They process the different elements within the soil and prepare the food for the plants. High level inputs of compost will help establish soil micro-organisms, so if your soil is not good make compost making your first priority and enlist the help of worms, fungi and bacteria to create a healthy soil in which you will grow your plants.

**(c) Soil Preparation**

A soil test provides the information you need to make the correct selection of the inputs you need for maximum soil fertility. A soil test tells you what minerals are missing and which ones are over-abundant and this is really important for growing healthy plants. Imbalances in soil nutrients mean you will have diseased crops that do not grow well. Trying to grow a lettuce when your organic soil is deficient in an important ingredient like silicon or calcium is a bit like baking a cake without flour. It just won't turn out right. When your soil is lacking some of the elements that are needed in tiny amounts will mean your lettuce will be less than perfect.

A soil test also tells you the level of organic matter in your soil and the ability of your soil to implement chemical changes that occur as soil nutrients are exchanged and distributed. Soil organic matter is a really important indicator of the number of micro-organisms because micro-organisms such as bacteria, fungi and nematodes are vital to soil health and plant health. Soil organic matter also determines the size of your worm population unless you continue to use harmful herbicides that kill worms and soil micro-organisms indiscriminately.

Having obtained your soil test you will know which elements you need to add. The soil laboratory you use (provided it is not one that is recommended by a company that produces chemical fertilizers) will advise you how to correct your mineral imbalances in the most sustainable way. Ideally your soil needs all ninety-two elements that exist on earth even though some of them will occur in minute proportions. These are called trace elements because you only find a trace of them in the soil.

Having discovered which elements are missing you then have to add them back ideally using natural fertilizers that break down slowly. We use things like soft rock, crushed basalt, crushed coal, powdered limestone, crushed diatomaceous earth and fertilizers made from seaweeds like kelp, or from fish. Blood and bone is also an excellent natural fertilizer.

By volume the most important three minerals are calcium, magnesium and potassium. Other essential elements are nitrogen, sulphur, phosphorus, silica and boron. The fertility of your soil will be determined by the element that is in least supply. For example, although you don't need a lot of boron, nothing works properly unless you have some and since boron leaches really quickly, this is an element you have to add continuously.

The best source of trace elements is anything that comes from the sea because the sea contains all the minerals that have been washed out of the organic soil over many centuries. Seaweed is an amazing source of minerals.

## (d) Building organic matter

We'd like it to be as simple as adding fertilizers in the right amount, but it is more complicated than that because the plants you grow can't always just take the fertilizers in the soil and use them. The fertilizers have to be made plant-available and this is where the micro-organisms and worms come in. Their job is to take the fertilizers you provide and turn them into plant-available food. Your job is to feed the micro-organisms and give them a good home! It's a two-step process.

By now you are beginning to get the picture. Growing profitably is about building a home for millions of creatures that live in organic soil but have been killed by using chemical fertilizers, herbicides and pesticides. Soil mismanaged as it has been, is generally deficient in organic matter, and lacks soil micro-organisms and worms. It is virtually dead: a medium in which to stand the plant up in but of little other value.

Growing profitably is about providing a good home for soil life and importantly, giving them what they need in order to thrive and multiply. When you attend to the basics, your plants will thrive and produce the most amazing abundance you can ever imagine.

Organic matter is the favourite food of soil micro-organisms and worms. Not only does it contain a whole range of mineral elements, it also contains carbon, which is essential for a healthy soil.

Organic matter comes from decaying vegetation and animal manures. You can just add organic matter like grass cuttings and leaves to your soil where it will break down but this process causes a lot of the very important element nitrogen to be used up in the decomposition process. A better way is to compost everything and then incorporate the compost into your soil. Compost is the end result of combining a whole range or organic material in a pile so that they break down and form a dark, carbon-rich, substance which micro-organisms absolutely love.

## (e) Fertility Maintenance

It takes quite a while before you build a system where all the elements you add to the growing area are recycled through the composting process. When you grow for sale, the plants will take up many of the elements you add in your fertilizer, so you have to keep adding an amount equivalent of what has left your garden.

There are three ways to maintain the fertility of your soil and to feed your plants.

1. Apply purchased fertilizers in a granular or powder form.

This is the most important method. Granules and powders have the best long-term impact in that they can effect a change in the soil mineral balance and soil pH. It may take a year for that impact to take effect, as the fertilizers have to be broken down into their different components by the soil micro-organisms.

2. Apply liquid fertilizer on the soil.

This has a much quicker impact on the plant but less long-term impact than granular fertilizers. The liquid fertilizers have been made soluble so they can be absorbed quickly by the plants or taken in by the micro-organisms.

3. Apply foliar sprays to the leaves.

This is the quickest way to provide plant food and is essential when essential elements are lacking in the soil. It is almost immediate in its impact and is therefore an excellent way to improve the size and quality of the current crop. Leaf tests can be used to identify any mineral deficiencies and foliar sprays can be used to correct them immediately.

If you are growing on a relatively large scale for profit it is recommended that

(i)     a spray unit for foliar praying of nutrients be used, and

(ii)    a fertigation system to be added to your irrigation system for effective and          efficient fertilization with liquid fertilisers.

It is highly desirable to use all three of the above methods. Whilst many people only apply fertilizers to the soil, this does not take into account the fact that different crops take up different elements out of the soil in varying amounts and heavy rain can leach minerals very fast.


Vegetables have a much shorter cycle than fruit crops and to save a crop or to ensure that it is of good quality size and quantity you need to keep feeding your plants regularly. Like humans plants benefit from regular feeding in small amounts, not large amounts infrequently.

You decide which fertilizers are needed based on your soil tests.

You decide what foliar sprays are required depending on what your leaf tests show.

When you are operating on a small scale you can use a watering can or maybe a backpack spray. When your operation becomes substantial in size you do well to instal irrigation systems with a fertigation unit, which is a method of putting liquid fertilizers into the irrigation systems so that fertilizers are distributed through your garden through sprays or pipes. Fertigation systems are huge timesavers if you are growing crops in ½ acre of more.

**(f) Weed Control**

Weeds are the bane of every organic grower. They must be controlled otherwise they will over-grow your crops and take up valuable nutrients.

You can use a form of weed matting that rots when it is incorporated into the soil. We prefer to mulch heavily between the rows and even between the plants. Mulch laid on top of the soil is gradually incorporated into the soil and adds to the carbon content so it is a multi-purpose strategy. It increases moisture retention, stops the soil becoming too hot when temperatures rise. Even with mulching it is necessary to hand weed particularly when plants are small.

# 5. Which crops will I grow?

## (a) Growing methods for the 12 crops.

I always use the same method for growing all vegetables. The entire garden is built up in a series of ridges and troughs. The ridges are where I plant my vegetables. The troughs are where I compost fertilizers, manures, mulch and lime in preparation for the next planting. One ridge and trench sequence takes up about 1 metre.

This method means that I always work three to four months in advance preparing the soil, which will be removed from the furrows and placed on the growing ridges immediately prior to planting. While this soil building process is going on, I am also providing a marvellous home for micro-organisms, worms and earth living creatures which are absolutely vital to have if you want to have healthy, disease and insect free vegetables. Most gardening books don't talk about the soil life upon which your plants depend. In fact, most commonly used gardening methods destroy soil life by advocating digging and cultivating which is totally unnecessary.

The method I use minimises weeds, removes the need to dig and enables me to remove vegetable stalks and old plants and **re-plant immediately** into unbelievably rich soil that I have been preparing for the previous 3 -6 months. It does require you to re-think how you approach gardening because it uses a method that is not widely known about and little understood.

The downside of this method is that mechanical cultivators cannot be used. The up-side is that they are not required.

I explain in detail how to create this unbelievably easily managed, fertile and productive garden environment and provide videos to show how it is done in my 12-lesson "Healthy Growing" training programme which you can read about by going to www.growinghealthyorganicfood.com. The programme is aimed at backyard gardeners and people who want to maximise production on small acreages.

In total, I have a vegetable garden that occupies about 1 acre. The proof that the strategy I advocate works unbelievably well comes from the fact that I have harvested every week from this one patch of land and I have grown three crops of vegetables every year.

Unlike most commercial vegetable growing areas, under this unbelievably intensive regime I have improved my CEC ratio from 15 to over 50. I have brought the soil organic matter levels to over 14% and have soil that is highly mineralised, balanced and full of all the minerals that plants need to grow really well. I have never used a poison spray on my vegetables. I've never had need to. The agronomist who does my soil analysis every year comments that vegetables grown in my garden must be unbelievably nutritious and full of flavour. They are. I cannot grow enough to meet demand.

So when I explain how to grow the vegetables that can make you a lot of money, you must realise that to do that you must have the skills and the knowledge to get your soil right and, even more importantly, to build its fertility, micro-organism population and humus levels as you continue to grow your vegetables. We can teach you how to do this. It is not something that happens overnight but you can plant within 6 months of starting to prepare you soil and, if you have to, you can start with infertile, unbalanced seemingly useless soil that doesn't seem to want to grow anything as long as you are prepared to start small and get it right.

Firstly, we take each of the selected crops and firstly show when to plant them and a summary of their spacing when planting. Secondly we go through each of the 12 crops in turn. Eight of them have seeds planted directly into the soil but there are four that are best grown first as seedlings and then the seedlings are transplanted out into the soil; these are capsicums, basil, spinach and broccoli.

## (b) Propagating seeds (growing from seedlings).

Broccoli, spinach (silver beet), basil and capsicum should all be transplanted into the garden area from seedlings. The reason for this is that it reduces the amount of time your vegetables are growing in the garden and it gives them a head start with regard to weeds. When seeds are planted into bare soil, weeds can outgrow them and smother them.

It is possible to purchase seedlings from a nursery but this is expensive. It is better to learn how to grow your own plants from seedlings.

To do this you need a polystyrene box which has holes in it, some newspaper, a bag of good quality potting mix, and a handful each of garden soil, lime, animal manure or compost and some all purpose fertilizer. Start by putting layers of newspaper in your polystyrene box. Mix together all the ingredients for your seed box and fill your box to within 2 cm of the top. Mark five or six very shallow lines in the soil. This is where the seeds go. You will be surprised how many seedlings you can grow in just one box and it is often a good idea to grow four or five different sorts of seeds in the one box unless you are growing on a large scale.

Sprinkle the seeds along the rows you have marked. Cover with a very light sprinkling of soil. Most seed box problems occur because people plant the seeds too deep and cover them with 1 cm or more of soil. Label your seed rows, water them and put them in a sheltered, sunny area to grow. Depending on the time of year your seeds will be ready to transplant within 3 - 6 weeks. Water daily and once a week mix up a very weak solution (1:100) of water, fulvic acid and soluble seaweed/fish fertilizer and water your plants with this.

## (c ) Spacing and when to plant seeds or seedlings.

| Tropical Crops. | Spacing In soil inches | Spacing In soil In cm. | Time To Plant |
|---|---|---|---|
| Buttonsquash | 15 | 38 | Su |
| Eggplant | 18 | 46 | Su |
| Capsicums | 12 | 30 | Su |
| Water melons | 18 | 46 | Su |
| **Temperate Climate Crops.** | | | |
| Basil | 12 | 30 | Su |
| Runner beans | 6 | 15 | Sp,Su |
| Beetroot | 4 | 10 | Sp,Su, Fa |
| Carrots | 3 | 8 | Sp,Su, Fa |
| **Cold Climate Crops** | | | |
| Radish | 18 | 46 | Sp,Fa |
| Mint | 12 | 30 | Sp |
| Spinach | 6 | 15 | Sp,Fa |
| Broccoli | 15 | 38 | Sp,Fa |

**NB**  su = summer, sp = spring, fa = fall or autumn.

# (d) Suitable crops for tropical climates.

## Button Squash (Patty Pan)

Button Squash are of the same cucurbit family as zucchinis. They are easy to grow but picking is a problem because the leaves are quite prickly and irritate the skin which means you have to wear long sleeves and long pants when harvesting these vegetables.

Button squash requires warm to hot growing conditions where plenty of water is available. They are best planted in late spring and into summer. There are many varieties of squash and they come in a range of colours including bright yellow, pale green, dark green and green and yellow stripes. I generally plant a variety of button squash called Scallopini, which is pale green because it has a higher yield than the more colourful varieties.

In areas with long warm summers, plant button squash from mid spring to mid-summer and plant every three weeks to ensure continuous harvest.

I plant my button squash seeds two to each hole. In the hole I place the seeds about 3 cm apart. Planting holes are 1 metre apart. When the plants germinate, I choose the healthier of the two small plants and carefully remove the weaker one without disturbing the root system of the healthier plant because button squash and zucchini resent root disturbance. Because the seeds are planted into a 6 cm deep layer of broken down manure and compost, minerals, lime and fulvic acid, which has been allowed to mature in the trench and is placed on top of the mound immediately prior to planting, no additional fertilizer is required at planting. As the plants grow, the roots extend into the trough area where the next crop's store of animal manure and minerals is breaking down. Except for a small  area around the seeds, the whole ridge and troughs are covered generously with mulch. After the seedling emerge, I cover the areas around the baby plant with mulch to prevent moisture evaporation and to control weeds. Watering with a mixture of fulvic acid, and a fish or seaweed liquid fertilizer mixed at the rate of 100 ml to 10 litres after the plants have produced their first fruit, prolongs the life of these these vine-like vegetable plants and encourages production.

Button squash is a vigorous grower and the trench and mound system provides an ideal solution to its habit of sprawling everywhere. In ideal conditions, production of 20 kg of vegetables per plant over a period of several weeks is quite possible.

The biggest problem with button squash is that the fruit grows unbelievably quickly when climate conditions are hot and moist. A 2 cm. button squash can become a 20 cm. giant, seemingly overnight. This means it is essential that you harvest daily to ensure you pick your button squash when they are still small and tasty with a thin skin and you have uniformly sized vegetables for sale. When squash is allowed to grow big, the skin becomes harder and this is good in that large squash last for many days but it does not sell well.

In wet conditions, button squash plants do get affected by powdery mildew, which slows down growth and production but doesn't affect the squash themselves. Excessive wet or heat also causes poor fruit set, which reduces production. It slows down growth and production but doesn't affect the squash themselves. Windy conditions can cause vine damage because these vegetables have long soft stems, which break easily when disturbed.

# Eggplant.

Eggplants love hot weather. They need 8 hours of full sunshine per day over a period of 60 – 80 days so it is a good idea to plant from seedlings rather than seeds to reduce growing time. They grow into large plants so leave ½ metre space between each one.

Plant into well limed, compost-rich soil and keep the soil around the eggplant moist by covering with a thick layer of mulch. Feed your eggplants once a fortnight with a combination of fish emulsion or seaweed, 1 teaspoon of borax (boron) and ¼ cup of molasses in a watering can of water.

They may require staking to protect from strong winds and also to support the weight of the fruit.
The leaves have thorns so wear gloves and use secateurs to clip the fruit from the plant.

# Capsicum.

Capsicums are semi perennials which are treated as annuals when grown commercially. They grow in frost free tropical and semi-tropical areas and need a 5-month growing period with temperatures over 25$^0$C to obtain high yields and quality fruit.

Capsicum seeds are quite difficult to germinate, particularly when temperatures drop at night. Plant the seeds about 1/3 cm deep in seed trays and leave in a warm sheltered place. If the growing seasons where you are growing capsicum is less than 6 months, you will need to germinate and grow seedlings for several weeks before you transplant. Transplant when the seedlings are between 10 and 12 cm tall. If you have one, use a greenhouse for seedling germination. If you don't have a greenhouse, cover your seed boxes with glass and place your boxes in 12cm deep manure, which will generate heat and warm the boxes. Another solution would be to germinate your seedlings somewhere indoors in a place that gets long hours of sunshine. As a last resort you could buy seedlings that have been grown in a nursery.

# Water Melon.

Watermelons require lots of space and three months of reliably hot (over 25 degrees C), sunny weather to grow and ripen. A lot of rain when the fruit starts to ripen causes it to rot and hot wet conditions are conducive to disease problems such as powdery or downy mildew which reduces production levels.

In tropical areas it is best to grow water melons in the drier winter season.

Watermelons do not grow from seeds taken from most purchased watermelons because these are likely to be hybrids. There are a lot of heirloom seeds available and if you use these, future watermelon crops can be grown from these seeds.

When planting watermelon prepare the growing area well in advance. Seeds should be planted in groups of 3 to 4 in several places within a 1 metre square of well-manured, composted, highly mineralized soil or along a 1 metre wide row. If planting in a row, plant 2 or 3 seeds about 20 cm apart. The area around the planting area does not have to be fertilized.

Make sure that the calcium/magnesium balance (see note below ***) in the soil is correct because deficiency of calcium causes blossom end rot. Melons with blossom end rot are not saleable. If you make your own compost, you could use the area where the compost-making operation is located. Alternatively fertilize the square or the row area and add lots of compost and animal manure and mulch heavily. It is not necessary to compost the animal manure as watermelon tolerates raw manure quite well.

The seeds are quick to germinate. Select the strongest of the plants and cut off the remaining, weaker plants. Do not pull them out as this disturbs the soil and the young watermelon plants do not like to be disturbed.

When the melon plants emerge, cover the area surrounding the plants with a layer of manure leaving a gap of about 10cm between the manure and the watermelon plant, and mulch the growing area really well. The manure will burn off emerging weeds and also provide on-going nourishment for the very heavy feeding watermelon vine.

When the plant grows, the male flowers emerge first and are much smaller than the female flowers. The first female flowers on each branch give the best fruit. Watermelons are Normally pollinated by insects. To be sure you can pollinate by hand removing the male petals and brushing the pollen laden stamen against the stigma in the centre of the female flowers.

It is time to harvest when the curly tendrils on the stem are totally dry and the light coloured patch on the watermelon where it has been lying on the ground starts to turn yellow.

N.B. The ideal calcium/magnesium ratio is generally about 7 to 1.***

# (e) Suitable crops for warm temperate climates.

## Basil.

Basil is an easily grown summer-growing herb that does not tolerate frosts. Most of the smaller leafed varieties such as purple and lemon basil require 6 to 8 hours of sunlight per day but the larger-leafed sweet basil will tolerate some shade.

Basil should be propagated in seed beds and transplanted in rows 20cm apart because basil grows into a small bush. It can be picked over several months provided that it is picked regularly and the flowers are removed. Allowed to grow without being picked, basil quickly becomes tall and spindly and the leaf size becomes smaller.

To grow successfully basil needs fertile soil with a pH between 6 and 7.5 and high organic matter levels. It requires regular watering at the base of the plant.

## Beans.

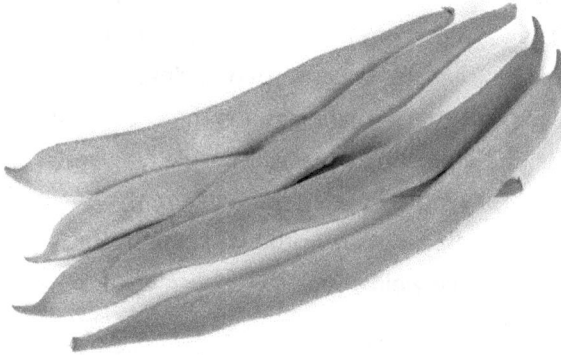

Beans are important in your garden. They add nitrogen to the soil through the action of nitrogen fixing bacteria, which live in bean root nodules.

Beans are really easy to grow so if you're a "beginner" this is a really good crop to start with because they grow in both cool and warm climates. Plant beans in the cooler months in warm climates, and in warm months in cooler areas. Planting every three weeks ensures a continuous supply.

Warm soils are required for germination, but excessive heat (over 30 degrees C) at flowering prevents pod formation. If you are worried that temperatures where you live are too high for ordinary beans, try snake beans, which have greater heat tolerance.

Depending on the variety you plant and the temperature at the time, beans take between 6 to 12 weeks to mature and be ready to pick. They can grow as a bush or a vine. Climbing beans can grow up to 3 metres in height and they need really strong support. Climbing beans, especially Purple King and Blue Lake are generally more tolerant of humid, rainy conditions than the bush varieties. Both high temperatures and excessive rain reduce yields.

The only way to grow beans is from seed. Sow the seed to a depth of about 5cm. Plant beans directly into the beds in rows. If you use the mounded system we recommend, plant two rows of beans along each mound, each row being as far apart as possible. Plant seeds 10 - 15 cm apart.

Plant into soil to which blood and bone or a good all purpose fertilizer has been added. Avoid adding animal manure, which is high in nitrogen.

Too much nitrogen causes excessive leaf growth. When your beans emerge (after about two weeks) and start to put out leaves, mulch the soil between the rows and between the bean plants. Ensure your soil has adequate levels of magnesium by spraying your plants with magnesium sulphate (Epsom salts) once or twice during the growth phase before flowers start to form. If you continually pick the beans, you'll extend the life of the plant and get more out of it.

The plants should be treated as annuals—once they've stopped producing, whip them out and chuck them in the compost so they can feed the next crop.

## Beetroot.

Beetroot are a really easy vegetable to grow and can be grown where temperatures are as low as 7 degrees C and as high as 24C. They do prefer temperatures between 16C and 18C. Autumn, winter and spring are the best growing times for sub-tropical and tropical areas as heat and humidity adversely affect growth.

It is easiest to plant beetroot seeds directly into the soil because they germinate quickly. Soak seeds in warm water for 1 hour before planting to speed germination. They can be transplanted when young as long as they are kept moist after transplanting. Beetroot likes deep, friable soil so growing on a mounded bed is ideal.

If your soil is heavy because it has a high clay content, add humic acid granules, lime, sand and/or crushed rock to open up the soil and allow oxygen to penetrate before you plant.

To plant, mark shallow furrows about 15 cm apart with a trowel. Place the seeds in the furrow and cover with about ½ cm of soil. Each seed is capable of producing 3 separate plants so it is a good idea to sow seeds 2-3 cm, apart. I sow my beetroot seeds much closer than most people recommend. The ones on the outside grow fastest allowing the slower maturing ones to be picked over a period of 4 to 6 weeks.

If you want large beetroot, sow the rows further apart and

be sparing with the seeds as you plant. When the beetroot plants emerge you can see where they are too close together. Weeds and seedlings emerge after two weeks. Pull the weeds out and at the same time remove beetroot that are too close to each other. Use the baby beetroot in salads.

When seedlings are 3 - 5 cm tall. side dress with an all purpose fertilizer such as blood and bone and mulch right up to the edge of the beetroot row with grass cuttings, straw or cane mulch. This retards further weed growth. A dilute mix of sea minerals and fulvic acid should be watered onto the plants when they have been growing for 6 and 8 weeks to give them a boost.

## Carrots.

Sow carrots directly into the soil. They do not transplant readily. They like deep, friable soil so growing on a mounded bed is ideal. Carrots don't like too much nitrogen so don't use animal manure before you plant.

If your soil is heavy because it has a high clay content, add humic acid granules, lime, sand and/or crushed rock to open up the soil and allow oxygen to penetrate.

The ideal growing weather for carrots is between 7 degrees C and 24C but carrots will germinate all year round even in extremely hot weather as long as they are kept damp. If the soil dries out, the seeds and seedlings "bake" in the heat. In hot dry weather water twice a day until the carrots are well established.

To plant, mark a very shallow furrow with a trowel. Many people have problems germinating carrots because they plant them too deeply. Cover the seeds with a very thin sprinkling of soil.

I sow my carrot rows about 15 cm apart, which is closer than is normally recommended. This means I don't get huge carrots, but I get lots and lots of medium sized ones. If you want large sized carrots, sow the rows further apart and be sparing with the seeds as you plant. Some people recommend mixing the seeds with sand, but I prefer to move along the row very quickly and allow the carrot seeds to fall onto the ground from a height of 1/2 metre. As they fall they spread out. When the carrots emerge you can see where the seeds have fallen too close together. Weeds and seedlings emerge after two weeks. Pull the weeds out when they are small and at the same time remove carrots that are too close to each other. Crowded carrots do not mature. Leave 1 cm. between each carrot plant. This is time consuming but not difficult if you do it when the weeds are tiny. If you let them get established, you have major problems. Side dress with an all purpose fertilizer such as blood and bone and mulch right up to the edge of the carrot row with grass cuttings, straw or cane mulch. This retards further weed growth.

Pick your carrots selectively. The ones on the outside of the row mature first. Pick them and allow the others time and space to grow.

# (f) suitable crops for cool temperate climates.

## Radish

---

Radishes are fast growing and extremely tolerant of a wide ($7^o$ - $32^o$C) range of temperatures. They are pest and largely disease free. Radish can mature in as little as 3 weeks.

Intermittent watering causes the roots to split and use of fresh manure, when preparing the soil, causes the roots to fork.

Seeds are direct planted about 2 cm deep and because they germinate and grow so quickly, can be planted among other, slower growing salad crops such as lettuce. Thin to 2 cm part when seedlings emerge if you are growing the red-skinned

French varieties.

Daikon, an oriental radish variety, has very deep roots and can grow up to ½ metre in length so the seedlings need to be thinned to 10 cm apart. Because the roots tend to push out of the ground, hilling of the soil is necessary to keep roots covered. Daikon are much slower growing than the red French varieties and take between 9 and 10 weeks to mature.

## Mint

Mint is an extremely hardy, perennial plant. It grows in full sunlight or in partial shade on well-composted, slightly acidic soils. Mint needs lots of water. It hibernates in very hot weather but can withstand frost. It is harvested by cutting all the stalks above the soil and it quickly re-grows. Mint can generally be harvested over a 6-month period. It goes into hibernation in hot weather and re-grows when temperatures drop.

Planting mint requires a source of rootstock, which can be gathered from existing plants. It is planted by hand, along shallow trenches, then covered with soil. Within a couple of weeks the mint stalks appear and the plant quickly spreads out laterally until, by late summer, a solid green mat is formed. Compost spread over the mint growing area helps maintain production.

Although mint is an extremely tough plant, erratic weather conditions will cause a form of rust. This can be controlled by cutting the mint back to ground level.

The major problem when cultivating mint is controlling weeds. Because it is a perennial plant, it is not possible to grow your crop, allowing it to shade out weed growth as you do with cauliflowers or potatoes, and then clean up the weeds when you harvest. With mint, harvesting involves cutting off the tops of the herb, leaving it to regrow. Weeding has to be a regular and on-going process, which has to be done by hand if you are going to ensure a weed-free crop. Your best weed minimisation plan involves using lots of mulch. Immediately after planting, thickly mulch everything except where the mint runners have been planted. Hand picking of any weeds that do emerge is necessary. When the final harvest occurs, re-mulch the whole area covering the soil with 3 -6 cm of mulch. Any form of straw will be suitable as is sugar cane or lucerne. When the mint plant starts growing again, it will be strong enough to emerge through the mulch layer.

In small gardens mint is a highly invasive plant.

There are over 3 thousand varieties of mint, but the best-known ones are spearmint and peppermint, which are used to flavour such things as toothpaste and gum. It is used as a herbal tea and mint oil has many medicinal benefits such as relief of irritable bowel syndrome. Penny royal, a native Australian non-edible mint variety, is used to repel fleas and bed bugs.

Mint is grown on a large scale primarily for oil. In Australia, requests from food processors for large quantities of fresh-cut mint on an on-going basis have been largely ignored because there are few growers producing large quantities of culinary herbs in Australia.
Large-scale mint production is best if combined with a steam distillation oil extraction process. Oil produced from mint is highly concentrated and can be stored for several years. A simple distillery method using a copper kettle and condenser pipe can extract 12 -15lbs of oil in a day.

Mint will drop in production levels over a 3-year period so it is a good idea to rotate your mint planting. Use four similarly sized beds at least one of which has been fertilized, manured and had compost added at least 3 months earlier and has been left covered with a thick layer of mulch.

In the first year plant mint in the prepared area and use the others for peas, beans or other green manure crops which will be mown and used as mulch on all four beds.

In the second year plant the second bed with mint and grow green manure crops for mulch on the remaining beds.

In the third year, use the runners from the mint that has been growing there to replant your third bed and re-plant the first bed with a green manure crop taking care to remove any mint runners as they emerge. Re-mineralise the first bed using generous inputs of an all purpose fertilizer, animal manure, cover it with mulch and leave it fallow for several months before planting legumes or green manure crops. In the period when the bed is lying fallow, test the soil of this area and rebalance the it with elements, including all the trace elements, that are deficient. Using this method you will be able to grow large quantities of mint while maintaining fertility of the soil.

# Spinach.

Spinach, which is often the name for the vegetable more properly called silver beet, is actually a variety of beetroot. There are many varieties of spinach. Silver beet is easier to grow than spinach, especially in sub-tropical regions and it is extremely productive because it can be harvested every week over several months. Soil fertility and nutrient availability is important because the more fertile the soil in which the spinach grows, the longer the growing and harvesting period. Spinach can tolerate pH levels from 6.5 to 8 in soils, which have good water holding capacity. This means it is important to have high (between 6 and 15%) organic matter levels because spinach's root system is very shallow and quite small compared to the size of the plant and the high levels of organic matter retain the water and stop the soil from drying out. Mulching is important because it also helps retain moisture.

Spinach can have green stems and light green leaves, white stems and dark green crinkly leaves or even yellow, pink and red stalks with red-tinted leaves. The more colourful varieties are generally referred to as chard. Miniature varieties, referred to as English spinach or baby spinach generally have smaller, softer leaves and grow into ground hugging plants. By comparison silver beet can grow into plants with leaves that are 40 - 50 cm in length.

You will find that when you grow spinach from seed it will take about 4 - 6 weeks to grow plants that are large enough to transplant safely. However, once transplanted the plants grow rapidly. When your spinach seedlings are about 3 - 4 cm tall, transplant your spinach into two rows, 20 cm apart and space the plants about 20 cm apart. When the plants are between 5 and 10 cm tall weed around the plants, use a liquid fertilizer, then mulch the ground well to maintain moisture levels and minimise weed growth. Fertilize every two weeks with a liquid fertilizer to maintain productivity making sure you water the fertilizer around the base of the plants and not the leaves.

Putting liquid fertilizer on the leaves will cause leaf blemishes.

Hot wet weather, water or nutrient deficient soil will cause plant to bolt and go to seed.

Harvest your spinach by cutting off the large outside leaves making sure you do not cut the growing stem. Under favourable conditions, spinach can be harvested weekly over a 3 - 4 month period.

## **Broccoli.**

Broccoli is a cool climate vegetable but it does surprisingly well in winter in semi-tropical regions. In cold climates it is a good idea to start propagating your seeds in autumn so that they can become well established before the cold weather slows down growth. When the temperatures increase at the end of the broccoli-growing season it is a good idea to harvest the broccoli heads just before they reach full maturity to avoid sun damage.

Non-hybrid varieties of broccoli tend to produce a large number of small heads. The broccoli with the large heads that we are accustomed to seeing comes from hybrid varieties, which produce a large head and then, 2 - 3 weeks later, five or six smaller heads. I grow in a semi-tropical climate and have found a hybrid variety called Atomic is extremely good.

Broccoli plants grow to 20 cm in height and can become top heavy and fall over. I plant my broccoli seedlings along 2 rows that are 20 cm apart. Within each row I plant my seedlings about 15 cm apart. This is very close planting because my aim is to maximise productivity rather than get the biggest possible heads. Planting this close means the heads that the broccoli produce are about 10 cm in diameter, rather than 15 - 20 cm diameter. Each plant produces about 5 secondary heads which when placed together are as large as the original head. It is only possible to do this if you have worked to develop a well-balanced, soil, which has a high (30 - 50) CEC, good organic matter (10%) and ample water and sunshine.

I plant on the outside boundaries of my ridges. This means that the broccoli plants spread over the trench area. When the plants are well established and are about 5cm tall, I mulch the whole area, after first removing the weeds. At this time I also give the plants a growth boost using the same diluted mixture of liquid kelp or fish emulsion and fulvic acid that I gave the baby plants. After picking, I fertilize the plants to ensure the secondary heads develop well.

As soon as the secondary heads are picked, I remove the plants and compost them so that I recycle the fertilizers that have been in the soil and have been taken up by the broccoli plants, back into the garden.

I work very hard to ensure my soil is nutrient rich and full of organic matter and micro-organisms. I have never had problems with diseases in broccoli. When I first started growing broccoli I had problems with white cabbage moths, but as I have improved my soil, the problems caused by cabbage moth caterpillars have lessened. When broccoli plants are rich in nutrients the eggs laid by the cabbage moth do not produce caterpillars.

# 6. Marketing.

## (a) Marketing Factors.

Marketing is a major consideration for any successful business. Marketing is the 20% of what you do that gets 80% of your results. The decisions you make here are vital to the success of your venture. The good news is that they are easy to change. If marketing is not working you can readily change direction and there are many marketing consultants you can seek advice from.

For the most part large growers continue to use the more conventional central market system, but complain that the prices they receive are low. They are concerned at the competition from imported food, which comes from countries where agriculture is subsidised or where labour costs are extremely low.

In some industries farmers have survived by becoming members of a local packing and marketing co-operative which, because of the size of its turnover, is able to negotiate with wholesalers and supermarkets from a position of strength, something they could not do as relatively small, independent producers.

### (b) Sell retail not wholesale.

Sales are much more profitable if you sell at retail prices rather than the normal wholesale markets. Selling at one weekly farmers' market or more markets is a good way to go. If there isn't one nearby, start your own like we did. However there is a limit to the volume that can be sold this way, so two options to increase sales are (i) to sell at several markets and (ii) to open your own retail outlet. The latter requires rent/lease or purchase of appropriate premises and staffing. A good option to investigate is setting up a retail venture with a cooperative with several farmers. This spreads the costs and also increases the range of goods on offer, as to be successful you need to provide enough products to attract the consumers to keep coming back. To do this you might have to buy in products not grown in your area or climate.

Our business has grown steadily. The major reason for our success is that we grow and sell quality food which is nutrient-rich. The alternative is commercially grown food which carries herbicides and pesticides or imported food. Our food is fresh. We generally pick produce today and sell today or tomorrow. Commercially grown food sold to supermarkets or through market agents often takes days or even weeks to get to the customer. Imported food takes months. Since nutrient content decreases with time this gives our fruit and vegetables a huge advantage.

The other major factor in our success is pricing. Most farmers sell at wholesale prices at the large city markets. We decided to sell at retail prices by setting the price ourselves by starting a local weekly farmers' market. We sell without the common premium for organic produce, because we buy much of our inputs at wholesale prices and sell most of our produce at retail prices. The difference is huge. We get 85% of the retail price (after costs of insurance, rent and marketing costs) compared to typically 20 to 25% of the retail price if you sell wholesale.

We became a wholesale distributor for our major fertiliser supplier which reduces our costs and also gives us an opportunity to make a profit selling fertilisers.

A clever marketing approach adopted by one farmer is to sell by mail! He produces garlic which is very light and has a high profit margin and lasts longer than most fresh produce. He can promote garlic on the Internet readily; anyone searching on "garlic" can find an advertisement to buy his fresh organic garlic.

Another idea is to check the seasonal price patterns for your produce and find how to gear your production to get the best prices.

**Diversity of Sales Strategies**

Conventional farmers rely on a centralised system of wholesalers. Over a number of years, this system has received a large amount of adverse publicity because of the perceived lack of transparency and resentment by growers who believe they are not treated fairly and honestly. Farmers have responded by establishing a

diversity of sales strategies which eliminate middlemen and to retain a much higher percentage of the value of their crops. These include:

• DIY sales being made through local markets or box delivery plans direct to consumers

• Internet and direct sales to a clientele that is built up over a period of years

• Personal contacts with local manufacturers

• Established wholesale distribution networks through co-operative packing and marketing systems

• Contracts with retail supermarket chains

• Direct export

• Value adding through processing.

## (c ) Incorporate DIY sales into your operation.

Many farmers  believe that their success is due to the fact that they have taken responsibility not just for the growing of crops but also for the marketing, and/or value adding of their produce.  The growing number and popularity of farmers' markets provides evidence to support this trend.

By selling locally, competition is limited to the produce available in nearby supermarkets or being offered by other growers.  People who purchase at farmers' markets and through connection to CSAs (community supported agriculture) do so because they want local, fresh, preferably organic produce.  CSAs are ways for produce to be delivered direct from the farmer to the consumer; usually this is done by supplying weekly boxes of fresh fruit and vegetables to private homes. Consumers like to be able to put a face behind the food they are buying and to be assured that the food they are buying has not had poisons sprayed on it. We sell to FoodConnect (a CSA) in Brisbane who deliver to 1500 homes  and they provide a reliable outlet for the larger volume produce that we grow too much of to be able to sell it at our local market. FoodConnect now operate in Sydney,

Melbourne & Adelaide plus some smaller Australian towns. There are CSAs in USA, Europe and Japan.

Another possible marketing solution is to create your own CSA by starting small. For example start by supplying 3 to 5 local families. Suggest the local families grow their own food and sell their surplus. Form a cooperative with some of these families &/or other local farmers to either (i) run a weekly farmers' market, or (ii) run your own retail greengrocer shop, or (iii) set up a warehouse or shed for produce to be brought into and arrange for someone to pack it into boxes and deliver it to homes.

You can bypass the normal wholesale market system by negotiating directly with any local manufacturers (such as food processors).

Some growers market their crops directly to the large supermarkets.   This is more worthwhile with organic production.

One farmer we know is developing a co-operative export initiative and is sending the harvest from 30 nearby farmers to China.

# 7.Step-by-step plan for success.

## (a) Examples of how to make $50,000 in 4 months.

1.Ensure water availability/irrigation?/water tanks?

2.Do a soil test.

3.Start composting

3.Prepare soil

4.Decide on which crops to grow.

5. Decide on how much space to grow each crop in.

6. Calculate seed quantities/order seeds (order at least two varieties of each crop).

7. Buy fertilizers

8. Buy mulch

9.Decide on tools & equipment required (trowels/forks/sprinklers/rideon & trailer/tractor?/spray equipment?

10. Prepare soil and beds in growing area

11. Decide whether you need a shadehouse or greenhouse

12. Decide on vehicle/trailer for transporting produce to market

13. Decide on shed or carport.

14. Decide on marketing method.

15. Assemble boxes, packaging & crates for taking produce to market.

16. Sow seeds & make sure you record in your diary the dates planted for each variety & each crop. Similarly record the dates you start harvesting & check their actual growing time.

Here's a specific example of how you can make $50,000 in 3 to 4 months in each of the three climate zones.

We will assume you sell at wholesale pricing.

| **Tropics.** | Growing time in weeks | (See note below)Kg production in 500 sq.metres | Wholesale price per kg | Dollar revenue |
|---|---|---|---|---|
| Patty pan | 7 | 4862 | 4 | 19450 |
| Eggplant | 10.5 | 2850 | 4 | 11400 |
| Capsicum | 10.5 | 3650 | 4 | 14600 |

| | | | | |
|---|---|---|---|---|
| Watermln | 11.5 | 4550 | 1 | 4550 |
| Totals | | | | 50000 |

Growing time is 2 to 3 months plus 3 weeks harvesting so that you sell a third of the production each week for 3 weeks and spread the labour of harvesting over 3 weeks. This achieves $50,000 income in 4 months. More could be achieved if you sell some at retail pricing or have organic certification which fetches better prices. This assumes you have a fairly good healthy balanced soil and adequate water or rain availability. The growing area required is 500 sq.metres per crop ie 2000 sq. metres or approx. half an acre.

N.B. 1 acre = 4047 sq.m. or 43,560 sq.ft.

1 hectare =2.5 acres= 10,000 sq.m.

### Note on production quantities used in these tables:

In these three examples I have used very conservative yields. You can check this by referring to the excellent book by John Jeavons (see references at the end).

Jeavons documented over 30 years of research in California and in his book he quotes yields achieved for many crops for beginners , good gardeners and excellent gardeners.

For 11 of the 12 crops used in this book I quote these yields in the table below. I then show the comparative yields used in the three tables for the three climate zones in this book. From this you can see that four of the yield figures I used are less than the beginner's figures recorded by Jeavons and seven are better than his beginner level but generally well below the "good" level. The 12th crop is mint which was not covered by Jeavons and here you can see I have used a yield that is far lower than any of the other eleven crops and one that is much lower than Jeavons' beginner level for basil.

| **From Jeavons** | Yield in lbs.per 100 q.ft. (approx 10 sq.m.) | | |
|---|---|---|---|
| | Beginners | Good | Excellent |
| Patty pan/squash | 75 | 150 | 307 |
| Eggplant | 54 | 108 | 163 |
| Capsicum | 68 | 136 | 204 |
| Watermelon | 50 | 100 | 320 |
| Runner beans | 30 | 72 | 108 |
| Beetroot | 110 | 320 | 540 |
| Carrots | 100 | 150 | 400 |
| Basil | 35 | 75 | 150 |
| Radish | 100 | 200 | 540 |
| Mint --not covered by Jeavons | | | |
| Spinach | 50 | 100 | 225 |
| Broccoli | 26 | 39 | 53 |

| From Jeavons | Yield in kg per 10 sq.m. | | |
| --- | --- | --- | --- |
| Patty pan/squash | 165 | 330 | 675.4 |
| Eggplant | 118.8 | 237.6 | 358.6 |
| Capsicum | 149.6 | 299.2 | 448.8 |
| Watermelon | 110 | 220 | 704 |
| Runner beans | 66 | 158.4 | 237.6 |
| Beetroot | 242 | 704 | 1188 |
| Carrots | 220 | 330 | 880 |
| Basil | 77 | 165 | 330 |
| Radish | 220 | 440 | 1188 |
| Mint --not covered by Jeavons | | | |
| Spinach | 110 | 220 | 495 |
| Broccoli | 57.2 | 85.8 | 116.6 |

**Yields used in this book.**

| Yield kg. per | 250 sq.m. | 100 sq.m. | 10 sq.m. |
| --- | --- | --- | --- |
| Patty pan/squash | 4862 | 1944.8 | 194 |
| Eggplant | 2850 | 1140 | 114 |
| Capsicum | 3650 | 1460 | 146 |
| Watermelon | 4550 | 1820 | 182 |
| Runner beans | 1950 | 780 | 78 |
| Beetroot | 6800 | 2720 | 272 |
| Carrots | 5700 | 2280 | 228 |
| Basil | 606 | 242.4 | 24 |
| Radish | 2600 | 1040 | 104 |
| Mint | 450 | 180 | 18 |
| Spinach | 3650 | 1460 | 146 |
| Broccoli | 1000 | 400 | 40 |

| Temperate zone | Growing time in weeks | Kg production in 500 sq.metres | Wholesale price per kg | Dollar revenue |
|---|---|---|---|---|
| Runner beans | 8.5 | 1950 | 7 | 13650 |
| Beetroot | 8.5 | 6800 | 2.5 | 17000 |
| Carrots | 10 | 5700 | 1.8 | 10260 |
| Basil | 7 | 606 | 15 | 9090 |
| Totals | | | | 50000 |

This result is similar to that for the tropical crops except the growing times are slightly better.

| Cold climate | Growing time in weeks | Kg production in 500 | Wholesale price per kg | Dollar revenue |
|---|---|---|---|---|

|  |  | sq.metres |  |  |
|---|---|---|---|---|
| Radish | 6 | 2600 | 7 | 18200 |
| Mint | 7 | 450 | 30 | 13400 |
| Spinach | 6.5 | 3650 | 4 | 14600 |
| Broccoli | 8.5 | 1000 | 4 | 4000 |
| Totals |  |  |  | 50200 |

This group has the shortest growing times so its possible to make the $50,000 in three months.

All three of these examples depend on achieving good production and the prices shown. These prices are conservative wholesale prices here in Australia and of course will vary both from season to season and from country to country. I have also allowed for paths in the area grown; in fact we advocate mounding the area and growing on the mounds or ridges leaving troughs on each side so effectively you grow in quarter of an acre and have a quarter of an acre for walking and picking!

Growing times will vary with the weather and with the different varieties of each crop. It is worth trying two or three different varieties of each crop to see which do best in your environment. Ask local gardeners or farmers which varieties do best in your location.

Want some more proof? Read my first book called "Growing Healthy" and subtitled "How I make over $100,000 p.a. growing fruit and vegetables organically". Also my wife has documented 18 case studies of different crops in her book called "Transition Farms". Since writing my book I did a two year research project analyzing the profitability of over 100 crops and I have documented the results in a training course called "How to double your profit growing". All three of these are available at www.growinghealthyorganicfood.com .

**Disclaimer**: the profit you make depends on the actions you take, your skill and experience as a grower, the weather and the prices you get.

**(b) Labour required.**

In Jeavons' main book (see references at end) he doesn't dwell on the labour (or hours of work) required to achieve the yields per crop. In a paper he wrote called "Cucumber Bonanza" he records the hours to achieve the results for cucumbers. Here he shows that takes 40 hours a week for 8 months to make a net profit of between $10,000 and $20,000 growing cucumbers on one eighth of an acre.  This confirms the dollars makeable on half an acre ie $40,000 to $80,000 p.a.

He makes the observation that there is a great deal of difference in the effectiveness and efficiency (and fitness) of different workers. His  labour estimate seems an excessive amount of time! Watering was a key time factor in his calculations and this can be automated with a sprinkler system which reduces his labour estimate quite a bit and clearly  experience & skill makes a great difference to the labour required.

 My own experience Is that it can take at least one good person per acre and probably two people to farm effectively.

# 8.Investment required.

Depending on the decisions you make, you may require:

A rideon & trailer $5,000 to $10,000

A shed or carport   $5000

Vehicle or trailer   $5000

Shadehouse or green house  $3000 to $10,000

Spray equipment $200 to $1000

Tools $300?

Fertigation unit $2000

Sprinklers/pipes/computer unit to control timing: $1000

Not everything has to be bought upfront; major items can be leased or acquired secondhand. You will require at least some tools and a watering can! But it is possible you could require an investment of say $20,000 or more. This has to be weighed up against the possible returns. These depend on the amount of space you plan to grow on. We make a healthy living on 3 to 4 acres. It is surprising how much can be grown in a small area.

One secret is to test different varieties of each crop that you grow. You will find that their growing time & productivity can vary significantly ( some varieties are better suited to other climates) e.g. different varieties of carrots' can vary from 10 to 20 weeks!

# 9. Conclusion:

If you like this report and want to learn more, visit my website www.growinghealthyorganicfood.com , where I offer (as course 2) the full results of my study of a comparative analysis of the profitability of over 100 crops including a step by step business model to maximize your return from growing in a garden or small farm. It also provides the use of a profitability calculator where you can input your own figures to calculate the specific profitability of a crop you grow in your climate, with your local pricing and local cost of labour and the growing time of the particular variety that you have chosen. Over 30 specific ways to improve your profitability are identified. This study is presented in the form of a series of 12 weekly lessons.

If you have trouble achieving the yields used in the examples, we also offer another training course with lots of videos on how to grow an abundance in a small area without any pests or diseases (and without using any pesticides or herbicides). Details are on the home page of the above website as course 1.

Best wishes for success,

Geoff Buckley.

December 2010.

P.S. If you have found this new report to be of value, I would really appreciate it if you could take a moment to provide a brief testimonial. It is always difficult to launch a product without testimonials. Send to me at buckleyg@bigpond.net.au.

References:

1. How to grow more vegetables by John Jeavons (Ten Speed Press).

2. Knott's Handbook for Vegetable Growers by D.Maynard & G. Hochmuth (J. Wiley & Sons).

**Disclaimer**: the profit you make depends on the actions you take. Results also depend on the weather and your skill and experience as a grower.